Receiving The Holy Spirit
With The Evidence of Speaking In Tongues

Receiving The Holy Spirit
With The Evidence of Speaking In Tongues

By

Steve B. Walters

Cover Design: Kimberly De Reuter/Sharon Walters

Graphics: Kimberly De Reuter

Editor: Anthony Buissereth

CROWNED WARRIOR
Publishing

2020

Receiving the Holy Spirit – with the evidence of speaking in tongues

First Printing: 2001

ISBN 979-8-6272639-7-7

Crowned Warrior Publishing
2939 Ericsson Street
East ElmhurstNorcross, GA 30092

Ordering Information:

Special discounts are available on quantity purchases by corporations, associations, educators, and others. For details, contact the publisher at the above listed address.

Dedication

This book is dedicated to the memory of Mother Dora Blackwell, founding mother of The Greater Evangelistic Churches of Christ of The Apostolic Faith, Inc., for her sincere love, service and faithfulness to the birthing of souls into the Kingdom of God

TABLE OF CONTENTS

Acknowledgements

To my dear wife Sharon for inspiring and encouraging me to write and for putting up with my late nights, early mornings and long hours at the computer. More than anything else for just being my wife and believing that I could do this before the idea of doing something like this ever entered my mind.

To the woman who gave me life, Sarah Walters, my mama.

To my pastor and Father in the Gospel, the late Apostle Lymus L. Johnson whose legendary exploits, as a national evangelist, (who's specialty was souls being born of the spirit) have motivated me do the same and write on this great subject.

To the late Mother Katie Bowens and Mother Ingrid Johnson whose knowledge, on the subject of altar work, has been a great resource.

To my daughters Katrina and Jenise and son Steven for being my best critics and for giving me great ideas

To our good friends Norm and Phyllis Allen founders of Oil of Gladness Ministries, for their knowledge, prayers and support.

To the many Altar Workers who, down through the years, have labored in the prayer room and have been used of God to keep the knowledge of Altar Work alive for those of us who now lift up holy hands without wrath and doubting.

What Makes This Book Different?

There are probably hundreds of books written on the Holy Spirit, but these books do not get into the specifics of how to receive Him. This book is totally dedicated to helping those who desire the baptism of the Holy Spirit to actually receive this baptism. It also deals with the ways one may receive, the hindrances of receiving, the process of receiving and what part altar workers may play in it. All of this is written in easy to understand language so that anyone can simply pick up this book, read it and instantly know how to receive the baptism of the Holy Spirit with the evidence of speaking in tongues.

This book does not pretend to be an all-inclusive and exhaustive study on the subject of "Receiving The Holy Spirit", but is in fact somewhat of a summary of the subject and is intentionally written that way. It does propose however, to get straight to the heart of the matter. And that is to aid believers in receiving the Holy Ghost with the evidence of speaking in tongues. Therefore, it is written in such a manner that it can be used in some of the following ways:

- As a guide to anyone who desires the baptism of the Holy Spirit
- As a course textbook in bible colleges
- In churches to train those that feel a call in their lives to Altar Work
- As an aid in preparing souls to receive the baptism of the Holy Ghost
- As informational reading for young ministers, laymen and Altar workers

Note: The words "HolySpirit" and "HolyGhost" are used interchangeably throughout this book.

There are many other areas where this may be used in the local church and bible colleges, which will become apparent as you begin to read and study this book. It is our desire, however, that Altar Workers are developed and souls are filled with the Holy Ghost the Bible way.

It is quite disheartening today to find that so many churches are turning away from laboring with souls until they have truly been filled with the gift of the Holy Ghost with the evidence of speaking in tongues as the Spirit gives them the utterance. Instead they are opting for the easy and fast way out. They are either teaching them how to speak in a tongue or telling them that they don't need to speak in tongues as the initial evidence of having the Holy Spirit. We've become so anxious for large numbers of converts that we've replaced true salvation with canned salvation, true worship with worldly entertainment, God's sweet anointing with a choreographed step and dramatic effect and finally effective altar workers with classes that teach sincere people how to do nonsensical babbling. There is nothing more important than helping souls receive the Holy Ghost! It is the one thing in the process of becoming born again that we are not personally in control of. We can decide to repent or be baptized in Jesus' name, but we cannot decide to fill ourselves with the Holy Ghost and actually do it. Only God can fill us with the Holy Ghost. It is also the one experience that guarantees a change in the individual. Sometimes the change may not be drastic, but we can say for sure that it's always a definite change! Numerous drug addicts, alcoholics and abusive persons, after several years in these conditions, have had a complete turnaround. What's so phenomenal about this is that the changes were instant, with no withdrawal, twelve step program or counseling. The experience further gives a precise moment of salvation. There are many people who consider themselves born again that have trouble determining if and when they were born again. This is not the case, however, with those that have received the Holy Spirit. These converts have no doubt whatsoever. To take this even further we've got to look at the fact that we are birthed into the body of Christ and the Kingdom of God through the baptism of the Holy Ghost (I Corinthians 12:13). All of this confusion forces us to ask ourselves some questions. What happened? What caused all of this? It seems that many of us have departed from the faith and are giving heed to seducing spirits (I Timothy 3:1). Instead of learning what it takes to help souls get beyond the hindrances of receiving the Holy Spirit, we've become frustrated with long tarry services (see the section on Altar Work). As a result of this neglect the art of tarrying for the Holy Ghost has greatly suffered. In many churches there are no qualified altar workers (see the section on Altar Workers) to work with souls until they come through with the baptism. Worse than that there's little or no documentation on the subject and in many cases a total lack of interest. Some have even labeled it outdated and no longer needed. It is our desire, however, to see more and more souls filled with the baptism of the Holy Spirit. The information contained within these pages has been proven to be a great help to those who want to be filled with the Holy Spirit with the evidence of speaking in tongues as the Spirit of God gives the utterance. It helps them prepare themselves prior to a tarry service, understand the process of receiving, knowing what might hinder them and how to get around these hindrances. We have found that when these principles, which are presented in this book, are applied that souls experience a reduction in the time it takes to receive the Holy Spirit and churches experience a definite increase in souls coming through with the baptism of the Holy Ghost with the evidence of speaking in tongues as the Spirit gives utterance. In fact, there was one case where a young man had tarried for the Holy Ghost for several years and decided to give up. He was so discouraged that he actually stopped going to church altogether. I had given his pastor's wife several copies of the book and she made sure he got a copy of it. Out of respect for his pastor's wife he read the book once. He then read the book again and then for a third time. That Sunday he went back to church and as he waited through the worship service he grew more and more anxious. He became fidgety as his pastor preached and wished that the pastor would hurry up and get to the Altar Call. When the Altar Call was made he rushed to the altar and before the pastor could pray or lay hands on him he was filled with the Holy Ghost and began to speak with tongues as the Spirit of God gave him utterance. Yes, this book teaches about tarrying for the Holy Ghost, but our MAIN FOCUS is that souls receive Him in any way the Lord sees fit!

Part One

Seekers

For The Promise is Unto You

One of the most exhilarating, breathtaking, electrifying and completely fulfilling things that you can ever experience is receiving the baptism of the Holy Ghost. I tell you words cannot describe the feeling of elation that you will have as the Spirit of the Lord just floods your soul. It's what the addicted person is looking for, but with all positive side effects, what the ambitious one is striving for, but more fulfilling, the thrill seeker seeks after, but far more thrilling, the dreamer dreams of but yet cannot ever imagine themselves obtaining. It is like reaching the unreachable, touching the intangible and seeing the invisible. In other words, it's indescribably delicious. And the most wonderful part of it is the fact that it's a part of your inheritance. That's right, it's been promised to you! Sadly, enough though, most people are not aware of this and are under the impression that only special people need to have this. It's sort of like a movie that I was watching with my two younger children where these two young ladies were summoned to the reading of the Last Will and Testament of a recently deceased friend. It turns out, to their utter surprise, that their friend had left them the bulk of his massive fortune while leaving absolutely nothing for his undeserving nephew. You may be asking, "Why did they receive this fortune?" It is because, before his death, their friend promised it to them in his will. They were not related to him in any way, shape, form or fashion. All they ever did was genuinely love, care for and teach him to once again have fun. He learned to enjoy life again. They made his last year of life the best year of his life. However, his nephew felt that they didn't deserve this blessing, but in spite of all of his protests and proclamations the promise was yet fulfilled. By the same token we can receive the Holy Spirit. For the Bible informs us that the Holy Ghost is a promise left to us of God. I find that today many describe this baptism of the Spirit as an additional blessing that some can have, but is not necessary for others. But the Bible tells us that it is promised to anyone that believes. In fact, it's promised to you, your children, your children's children and as many as our Lord God shall call (Acts 2:39). The problem is that someone has either neglected to summon us to the reading of the will or has intentionally left that part of the will out! That's right I'll say it again. You too can receive the Baptism of the Holy Ghost with the evidence of speaking in tongues as the Spirit of God gives the utterance. It's been promised to you. Let's take a look at the scriptures that refer to the receiving of this blessing:

Matthew 3:11: John said that Jesus SHALL baptize you with the baptism of the Holy Ghost.

Luke 11:13: Jesus says that the Father WILL give the Holy Spirit to them that ask Him.

John 7:38: This scripture shows Jesus telling the people that the Holy Ghost SHALL flow out of the bellies of those that believe on Him.

Acts 2:38: Peter declared that those who have repented of their sins and have been baptized in the name Lord Jesus Christ SHALL be filled with the gift of the Holy Ghost.

Did you notice where it says shall or will? This indicates a promise. It means that it's yours. You are entitled to it. Please allow me to be a little southern. Shall means that you SHO-NUFF WILL! I am telling you that you most certainly will receive this baptism. The scriptures did not say you might, perhaps, maybe or it's a possibility. It emphasized a definite SHALL and WILL. In other words, there is no doubt about it at all. So come on and take hold to your inheritance and receive the promise. Let me end this chapter with this. Are you one of those who are aware that there's something else in God that you are missing? That you didn't get every-thing you were supposed to get? Well guess what? You do not have to re-main that way because what is missing is the baptism of the Holy Ghost with the evidence of speaking in tongues as the Spirit gives the utterance. Go ahead and receive this wonderful gift. After all it's been PROMISED TO YOU!

Chapter Two

You Receive By Faith

Text: Ephesians 2:8

It is my sincere desire, in writing this book, to make it very clear to the reader that it is in no way difficult to receive the Baptism of the Holy Ghost. It is extremely simple and easy. Receiving the Holy Ghost is like receiving an unseen gift. For when someone tells you that they've brought you a gift you react in the following ways:

You believe it before you see it.

You give thanks prior to receiving it.

You rejoice and get happy before you know what it is.

You sometimes don't feel worthy of it.

You never feel that you have to do something special before they will give it to you.

You with a smile and a feeling of expectation reach out your hands and arms to receive it.

It is vitally important for you to understand, as you tarry, that the only thing you have to do is Receive. Just like a long lost friend at your door. You receive them by opening wide your door, arms or heart. If you do this to the Holy Ghost, do you know what will happen? He will come in and totally flood your soul with His Spirit. So open up your heart and receive Him, for by grace are ye saved through faith. Do you understand that you do not have to work for a gift? There's no measuring up, earning the rights to, pleading, begging or even coaxing the Lord to fill you with this gift. It's a gift. I realize this sounds oversimplified, but it really is that easy. There is no impressing anyone. Just receive by faith. You cannot see the Holy Spirit. Therefore, you must receive Him by faith.

Note: If you are utilizing this chapter as an outline for a lesson for teaching people how to receive the Holy Ghost, then at this point you should have testimonies from at least three people from different age groups who have already experienced the Baptism of the Holy Ghost. They should tell of what they experienced during the process of tarrying and of the very moment they realized they were speaking in tongues. After this you can make your final remarks and begin your tarrying service.

Chapter Three

The Methods & Process of Receiving

Text: John 3:5, Acts 2:4

Jesus told Nicodemus that if one is not born of the Spirit he CANNOT enter into the Kingdom of God. With this being as crucial to our eternity as it is; I find it quite unfortunate that there is so much confusion and debate regarding this subject. Some say there is a difference in the baptism, filling and receiving of the Holy Ghost. Then there are those who say you need to speak in tongues as the evidence of it and others say you don't. One group says you simply conjure up the Tongues from your belly and start speaking. While another group says that you can only Speak in Tongues as the Holy Ghost gives you the utterance. This chapter is designed with the purpose of bringing closure to these arguments and ultimately to show you how to receive the Holy Ghost for yourselves.

The Difference in The Baptism, Receiving and Filling of The Holy Ghost, Or Is There A Real Difference?

Let us take a careful look at the scriptures that use the many references to someone having an experience with the Holy Ghost as described by the words given above. In Matthew 3:11 John the Baptist tells of a Baptism of the Holy Ghost and a Baptism of Fire, that was to be given by Jesus. Jesus says in John 7:38 that there would be a flowing from our bellies, which the scripture helps us to understand that he was speaking about the HolyGhost that the believers would receive. Shortly before Jesus ascended back into Heaven He breathed on His disciples (John 20:22) and told them to receive the Holy Ghost. It must be understood that this is the same occasion where Jesus says "And, behold, I send the promise of my Father upon you: but tarry ye in the city of Jerusalem, until ye be endued with power from on high (Luke 24:49)." What promise? It is the promise of us having the gift of the Holy Ghost (John 7:39). So if He breathes on them and tells them to receive and then says tarry here until you are endued, it seems quite evident that they did not receive the HolyGhost at that moment. I think we should also look and see what happened when they did. We notice that in Acts 2:4 where they have an actual experience with the Holy Ghost that the Fire is also present. This certainly sounds like what John the Baptist mentioned earlier with the exception of how it's described. The Baptism of the HolyGhost is described as a filling of believers and the Baptism of Fire is described as sitting on them. With careful examination of these different terms and the occasion in which they were used; it is very easy to see that different terminology is being used to describe different aspects of the same experience. You can do the same thing to describe how you felt after a long journey and finally arriving at your destination. You can be relieved, happy, excited, exhausted etc. Therefore, there is absolutely no difference in being baptized, filled or receiving the Holy Ghost. There are just different terms used to describe aspects of the same experience.

How Do You Know If You've Received The Holy Ghost?

The Bible teaches that you need to be born of the Spirit to get into the kingdom of God (John3:5). It also teaches that "… if any man has not the spirit of Christ, he is none of His" (Romans 8:9). In other words, without the Holy Ghost you are not saved. Let's face it. The above scriptures teach us that if you do not have the spirit of Christ (The Holy Spirit/Ghost), then you don't belong to him. They also teach that we will not be able to enter his kingdom. How could the church, which is the body of Christ, not belong to Him and not be in His kingdom? Now that we have demonstrated to you how crucial it is for you to have the Holy Ghost, we also want you to be able to identify/recognize when you've received the Holy Ghost. We know that the first time that the disciples received the Holy Ghost was on the Day of Pentecost; so let us look at what it says. "And they were all filled with the Holy Ghost, and began to speak with other tongues, as the Spirit gave them utterance (Acts 2:4). According to the scripture when they received the Holy Ghost for the first time (which sets a precedent) the disciples Spoke in Tongues. Not only did they speak but, they did so as the Spirit gave them the utterance. We could simply stop right here and be satisfied with Speaking in Tongues as the initial evidence and that they spoke only as the Spirit gave utterance, but since there is so much of a controversy surrounding this we need to look further to prove the point more conclusively. In Acts 10:44-46 we see that the Hebrews realized that the people of Cornelius' household had received the Holy Ghost just like them (remember the precedence?) when they "heard them speak in tongues'. Wait a minute. What was the reason they knew the Gentiles received the Holy Ghost also? They heard them speak in tongues! Then after that Peter, in telling the other apostles, etc about the event, said that the Gentiles received the Holy Ghost just like they did (there's that precedent thing again) at the beginning (Acts 11:15,16). What happened in the beginning? They spoke in tongues! When the disciples of John, the Baptist, received the Holy Ghost (Acts 19:6) guess what happened? They spoke in tongues! In Samaria Simon the Sorcerer noticed that when the Apostles laid hands on the people they received the Holy Ghost. How did he know, since it did not say what happened? It may not have said what happened, but it did mention that he noticed that the experience took place. It's not hard, based on all of the other evidence, that what he saw was the people speaking in tongues. To further emphasize that they did not do this on their own; we must take into consideration that Peter and John were sent for the purpose of these converts receiving the experience (Acts 8:17, 18). So let's make this perfectly clear. Speaking in Tongues is not the only evidence, but it is for certain the initial evidence of one receiving the Holy Ghost and furthermore the tongues are not conjured up. It is the Holy Ghost that gives you the utterance. How do you know if you've received the Holy Ghost? When you've spoken in tongues as the spirit of God gives you the utterance. Now let me explain something to you about speaking in tongues. Sometimes we think that when the Lord speaks through us in tongues He's going to take over my tongue in a forceful manner. However, this is not true. He never forces your tongue, but uses your tongue in such a gentle and apparently natural way that in most cases you will not know the exact moment that you started speaking in tongues. It is not abrupt, but gentle, so don't get caught up with getting the tongues or how the Lord will take over. Just enjoy His presence when it comes. Just remember that you will recognize that you have the Holy Ghost when you begin to speak in tongues as the spirit of God gives you the ability to do so.

Confusion Over Speaking In Tongues

It seems that from its inception at the Day of Pentecost there has been confusion over speaking in tongues. Ranging from the idea that people who spoke in tongues were drunk, demon possessed, whether it is the initial evidence of one receiving the Holy Ghost, the idea of them being out of order because there was no interpreter and finally the concept of the speaker being able to control and conjured up the tongues at will. Much of this confusion can easily be cleared up when you understand how God has used speaking in tongues. There are at least three different ways that are demonstrated in the scriptures in which God uses speaking in tongues. The first is the "Initial Evidence" of one receiving the Holy Ghost (see "How Do You Know If You've Received The Holy Ghost." The second way in which God uses speaking in tongues is known as "Praying in Tongues" (I Corinthians 14:14,15). This takes place when you are praying and the Holy Spirit takes over and prays through you in tongues on your behalf strengthening you in areas where you may be weak (Romans 8:26). Finally, the third way that has been demonstrated where God uses speaking in tongues is known as the "Gift of Tongues." This is used to edify the body of Christ through a message of prophesy with the use of an interpreter (I Corinthians 12:28-31). The correct order and use for this wonderful gift is given in I Corinthians chapter 14 verses 27 & 28. When you clearly understand the different ways in which God uses speaking in tongues you will find that all confusion on this subject quickly dissipates.

Methods of Receiving The Holy Ghost

Receiving this precious gift has been demonstrated, in the scripture, by at least three different ways. The first is called Tarrying. The word Tarry simply means to wait. In the case of receiving the Holy Ghost, it's a waiting with anticipation. While the disciples were waiting on the Lord to fill them with the HolyGhost we believe they were praying and praising the Lord. The second is with the Laying on of Hands. This was demonstrated when Peter and John laid hands on the Samaritan disciples. When hands were laid on them these people received the Holy Spirit. I remember experiencing this early in my ministry. A guest preacher at the end of his sermon concluded without giving the invitation. My pastor, Apostle Lymus Johnson, told me to get up and do the Altar Call. When I stood up and gave the invitation a young man came to the altar. I asked him what he desired from the Lord and he said, "I want to receive the Holy Ghost." I laid my hands upon him and prayed that he would receive and the presence of the Lord came upon him and he began praising God. Within seconds there was a beautiful flow of tongues emanating from his lips.

What a wonderful experience. Finally, the third way of receiving is characterized as the Holy Ghost Falling upon you. This occurred when Cornelius's household was listening to Peter preach. While he preached the Holy Ghost Fell on them that heard the word. I have witnessed this happening when Apostle Lymus Johnson was preaching one Sunday morning. He was preaching on receiving the Holy Spirit and in the midst of his preaching we heard someone begin speaking in tongues. When we looked to see who it was we realized that this sister had never received the Holy Spirit and was being filled as the Apostle preached. However, the most common way documented in which people have received the Holy Ghost is through the method of tarrying and since this is the method most used we will take this method and explain this process in more detail.

The Process of Receiving The Holy Ghost

There are three stages that one normally goes through when tarrying for the gift of the Holy Ghost. If you understand and recognize these stages, it will reduce the time it takes and make it much easier for you to receive the Holy Ghost. The stages are Worship, Conviction and Refreshing.

Worship

As we stated earlier the word Tarry means to wait and we believe based on Acts 1:14 ("These all continued with one accord in prayer and supplication") that while they were tarrying they were also praying and praising God. Also in Acts 2:1 (...they were all with one accord in one place...), where they actually had the experience, it seems to indicate that there was a continuance of the same. We have used the practice of worshiping and praising God by calling on the name of Jesus (Acts 2:21 'whosoever shall call on the name of the Lord shall be saved.). This is not a begging or pleading to God to give us His GIFT that he has promised, but simple worship that says thank you. Some churches do not teach the seeker to call on the name of Jesus. Instead they tell them to say Hallelujah. This is perfectly fine. Please understand that this not a chanting or emptying of your mind to get into some heightened state of awareness or frantic emotional state, but a simple worship that says thank you for your gift of love. The idea is to bless the Lord, pour your love upon the Lord and thank Him in advance for this marvelous gift. It is an act of faith. So whether you are calling on the name of Jesus or saying Hallelujah just worship and praise the Lord with all of your heart. As the result of worshiping and praising Him we begin to feel his presence for Psalms 22:3 teaches us that the "Lord inhabits the Praises of Israel." What are we saying? We are telling you that when you praise God; His Anointing (presence) comes upon you, which is what you want to happen. The purpose of Tarrying in this manner is to bring ourselves into the presence of the almighty so that He may come into us and fill us. What should we do when the anointing comes? Enjoy the experience and continue your worship of Him, for at this point, you are entering the Holy Place.

Conviction

Convict means to find guilty. After you've entered the presence of God (the Holy Place) a sense of how Holy He is comes over you. At the same time, you may also experience a sense of how unholy and unworthy you are. This is not necessarily a feeling of being criticized or rejected, but more of a knowledge of our true condition accompanied with a knowledge of God's mercy. The Prophet Isaiah experienced this very same thing in Isaiah 6. In most cases you begin to cry and experience a sorrow accompanied with a deep need to repent. Sometimes you may start crying. There's nothing wrong with this. Allow it to happen. Lift your hands and surrender to the Lord. Accept the fact that you are experiencing this because the Lord is present and ready to fill you with his sweet Holy Spirit. Allow Him to do just that by receiving/accepting that this is exactly what is taking place. Please understand that the most important part of this stage is for you to REPENTENCE & RECEIVE. Go ahead and repent within your heart, forgive others and confess to Him from within while continuing your outward worship of His wonderful name. You can simply say in your heart, "Father I'm sorry and I give it all to you. Thank you for your forgiveness." Don't get caught up with your emotions and stop tarrying. As you repent thank Him for His mercy and forgiveness; for He is simply cleaning out the temple (you) before He moves in. For your own sake do not quit here because you are just about to enter the Most Holy Place.

Refreshing

To refresh means to give new strength or energy to someone or something; to recreate, revive after fatigue, want, pain or the like. Let me tell you, after the Holy Ghost moves in, you are in every sense of the word refreshed (Acts 3:19). Having said this, I must also admit to you that I cannot give you a full description of how you will feel because this is something that is incomparable. Enjoy this experience. There is absolutely nothing for you to do but enjoy the Lord because He has completely taken over at this time. This comes automatically when you've handled Conviction correctly. Go ahead and praise Him! Enjoy the Shekinah Glory of God flooding your soul. About this time, you are so filled with the presence of God that you may not realize it, but you are speaking in an unknown tongue (unknown to you). Don't try to change what's coming out of your mouth. The Lord has your tongue. Allow Him to speak through you. You are now in the Holies of Holies (the Most Holy Place).

Gregory's Experience

It was an early Saturday morning when I was awakened by a phone call from Gregory. We previously met in a bookstore where I was having a book signing. After conversing with him I gave him my card so that he could contact me if he had further questions. Greg had been trying to reach me for a couple of weeks, but unfortunately we kept missing each other. Consequently, he was now calling me early on a Saturday morning. He indicated to me that he had some questions and when I inquired as to what his questions were he responded with, "I want to receive the Holy Ghost." I explained to Greg that he could receive the Holy Spirit at that very moment and as I was speaking to him the Holy Spirit told me that he could receive it over the phone. I knew it was the Holy Spirit because I was just going to encourage him and go right back to sleep. Hey what do you want? It was the Sabbath. I told Gregory that I was going to pray with him a prayer of repentance and after that he should begin to worship the Lord by calling on His name, Jesus, while inwardly thanking the Lord for filling him with the Holy Ghost in advance. I also told him that when he began to feel the presence of the Lord to enjoy it and continue to worship him. Well as it turned out we prayed the prayer of repentance and Greg tried to begin his worship, but as he began the presence of the Most High overshadowed him and he began to beautifully speak in tongues as the Holy Spirit gave him utterance. It was so wonderful. He spoke in tongues for a good ten minutes before I awakened my wife, who was still asleep in the bed beside me. Still groggy she said, "What's going on? Who is that speaking in tongues over the phone?" I told her it was Gregory, one of the young men we recently met during one of our book signings. We rejoiced in the Lord along with Greg. Finally, I stopped Greg and asked him how he felt and he said, "I feel so good!" and began speaking in tongues all over again. He went on to tell me that as he began to worship all of a sudden the entire room became bright with this light. He further explained that all of his window shades were completely down so that no light could come in. He then told me he felt the Holy Ghost come all over him and yes he said that he realized that he was filled with the Holy Ghost after he heard himself speaking in tongues.

Chapter Four

Hindrances

We have seen many receive the precious gift of the Holy Ghost. While some receive the Holy Ghost relatively quick, others seem to have hindrances and take more time. In our experience we have come to recognize and understand some of the things that hinder souls from receiving the Holy Ghost. Therefore, we have listed some of them in an effort to better prepare souls prior to the tarry service so that they will receive the Holy Ghost with the fewest hindrances possible.

Not Asking

The Bible teaches that God will give the Holy Ghost to them that ask Him (Luke 11:13). It also says that He knows what we want before we ask (Matthew 6:8) and yet He tells us to ask. The Word also teaches us that we have not because we ask not (James 4:2). So go ahead and ask; for He "… will give the Holy Ghost to them that ask."

An Unrepentant Spirit

Let's look at what repentance is: It is feeling sorrow for what you've done, turning away from sin and the dedication of yourself to the changing for the better by surrendering your will to God. The reality of the matter is that you cannot expect God to give this wonderful gift (which gift He is) to you when you are not willing to surrender to Him. In fact, God will not even acknowledge you if you don't repent of your sins. Psalms 66:18 says, "For if you regard iniquity in your heart, the Lord will not hear you." On the other hand, the Word also says "… a broken and contrite (repentant) spirit, O God, thou wilt not despise" (Psalms 51:17). So make yourself undeniable by repenting.

Pride

One of the greatest hindrances you can have while tarrying is pride. It will have you worrying about anything from how you look, who's looking at you, how you sound to how loud you sound. This totally annihilates your concentration and your chances of receiving the Holy Ghost. Forget about all of those things and think about your salvation. As we often say "let go and let God."

Doubt

Doubt is simply having disbelief in what you're doing and anything done in doubt is almost always not done wholeheartedly. To tarry is to wait with anticipation of receiving the Holy Ghost. Therefore, you cannot tarry and receive anything when you do it in doubt. This is called being double minded and the scriptures tell us that we should not expect to receive anything from God in this condition (James 1:6, 7). Remember what the scripture says about you receiving the Holy Ghost. It says "you shall!

Fear

All types of fears can come upon you when tarrying. It can range from fear of embarrassment to fear of rejection. The only reason fear comes is to hinder you from receiving the Holy Ghost. The scripture tells us that God doesn't give us a spirit of fear (II Timothy 1:7), so understand that this spirit of fear should be rejected and not allowed to interfere with you receiving the Holy Spirit. Sometimes the fear comes from a lack of understanding as to what is going to take place. I often hear people refer to someone receiving the Holy Ghost in a negative manner. They say things like, "They caught the Holy Ghost" or "They put the Holy Ghost on them." They say this as if it is a disease or some spell or incantation. It is further complicated by the idea that some evil spirit is going to come inside me. Misconceptions like these make receiving the Holy Ghost sound spooky. It is nothing like that at all. This is not a ghost; spook or spell being cast upon you. This is the Lord Jesus Christ himself coming inside you to live in you and be with you as a helper, teacher and guide (John 14:16-18, 26). To bring it to its simplest form we can compare it to entering into an atmosphere that changes your mood. Have you ever walked into a room and felt a sense of peace, sadness, or uneasiness? Guess what? The spirit of peace, sadness or uneasiness entered into you when you stepped into that room. Is this a strange thing? No it isn't. The difference is that you are familiar and comfortable with those experiences. Thinking that receiving the Holy Spirit is in its very essence so different than these previously mentioned experiences brings a sense of uneasiness and fear. FEAR is just

False Evidence Appearing Real. So refuse the fear and receive what God gives: power, love, a sound mind and the Holy Ghost.

Involvement in Witchcraft, Horoscopes, Roots, Tarot, Psychics, Hypnotism, Ouija Boards, Dungeons and Dragons etc.

(Text: Exodus 20:3, Deuteronomy 4:19)

If you've been involved in anything of this type, then you have given the enemy a right to inhabit you. These things, demons, must be removed from your life. The sin must be confessed, repented of and renounced. You must declare Jesus Christ as your Lord. Pray with a skilled altar worker and use the Renunciation and Affirmation letter (found at the end of this chapter) as your confession.

Lack of Determination

The BIGGEST and most common factor that people, who have received the Holy Ghost, share is a firmness of mind to receive him. More than anything else, they mostly say that they were determined to receive the Holy Ghost at that moment. Something quite special often happens when someone has a determination. They usually will not take no for an answer and with that attitude they are rarely denied. So take the hint and get determined.

Not Receiving

I have seen a lot of people, who have waited for God to do all of the work, and go home unfulfilled. God's job is to give the gift and your job is to receive the gift. Whenever someone is giving something to you, there must be a corresponding action from you for it to be considered received by you. In other words, you've got to hold out your hands and take what's being given to you or otherwise it will not be received. This is what needs to be done to receive the Holy Ghost. What I mean is this: when the anointing is all over you, then you need to believe and accept that the Lord is doing His job. When He does this simply reach out with your heart, believe and welcome, in your mind, the fact that He is filling you. Go ahead get happy. Embrace this wonderful gift.

Unforgiveness and Feeling Unworthy

The scripture teaches us that if we don't forgive, then the Lord will not forgive us (Matthew 6:19). Consequently, harboring unforgiveness has the ability to preclude you from receiving the Holy Spirit. Please understand that forgiveness does not mean that wrong things that have been done to you are acceptable. That's not what it means at all. What it does mean however, is that you are no longer looking to extract vengeance on the perpetrator. For those that need further consolation regarding this; I'd like to remind you that the scriptures teach that vengeance belongs to the Lord and He promises to repay (Romans 12:19). Furthermore, Galatians 6:7 reminds us that we will reap what we sow. In other words, forgive and allow God to take care of the rest. What I have found to be quite interesting is though is how we can find it so difficult to simply forgive ourselves. This tragedy has caused many to feel unworthy of God's wonderful gift of grace. The beautiful thing about this gift is that our worthiness has nothing to do with us receiving it (Ephesians 2:8). Nevertheless, there are those who are hindered by this when it comes to receiving the Holy Ghost. I recognized this when I was invited by a pastor friend to come hear the revivalist at his church. When I arrived he introduced me to him and informed him about my book on receiving the Holy Ghost; highly recommending it. This man of God responded to him with, "I'll read it and if I find that is has anything good in it, then I'll buy it." I simply sat there and smiled. Shortly after the service began the Lord spoke to me saying, "He's going to try you, but fear not. He's not really trying you he's trying Me." I sat there and totally enjoyed the sermon and at the end the revivalist made an Altar Call. As a minister I usually don't step into anyone's Prayer Line/Altar Call uninvited. I was taught it was disrespectful. Therefore, when he made the Altar Call, I stayed there on the pulpit and prayed over him for guidance as he ministered to the souls that came up for prayer, salvation etc. As I was standing there watching him work, for a considerable amount of time, with a young woman who wanted to receive the Holy Ghost he turned around and beckoned for me to come. The Lord again reminded me that it was not me being tested. I walked over to him and the young woman and he looked at me and said, in somewhat of a challenging tone, "Go ahead!" Saints, writing a book on receiving the Holy Ghost does not mean that you have the power to give someone the Holy Ghost. We tend to miss the mark with people in that we equate the move of God with the person's ability and not the fact that they are just yielded vessels being used of God. We are all just pencils in the hand of the master artist. The only one who can give the Holy Ghost is Jesus. Yes, I know. You want to know what happened. Well as I approached the young woman the Lord spoke these words, "Tell her to forgive HERSELF! Tell her to forgive herself for the things she allowed." As I laid hands upon her I whispered to her what the Lord told me. The Lord then told me to step back. I took two steps back and the young woman began to, as if in slow motion, fall to the floor. As she did so she began speaking in tongues. It was one of the most beautiful things I'd ever seen. She sat there on the floor, tears streaming down her face with a look of pure joy and peace. I thought to myself, "I will beautify the meek with salvation (Psalms 149:4). You see she was holding on to unforgiveness. In this case she had not forgiven herself and as soon as the Holy Spirit revealed this to her she was set free and received the Holy Ghost with the evidence of speaking in tongues as the Spirit gave her utterance.

The Renunciation And Affirmation

In many cases we have, knowingly and unknowingly, allowed or have had placed upon us ungodly attachments. These attachments can become a definite hindrance and severe burdens in our lives. The prayer below is designed to remove such attachments. Please sincerely and prayerfully read it and in doing so you will receive a tremendous deliverance from God:

In the presence of the almighty and only wise God I assert that I am a child of God redeemed with the blood of the Lord Jesus Christ (Romans 6:3 -11). I recognize Him only as my Lord and Savior and unequivocally renounce Satan as my lord and god. Since my only hope for eternal life is in the finished work of Christ on Calvary, I now forsake and disavow all the sins of my ancestors in their workings, effect or claim upon me. Since I have been delivered, through the blood of Jesus Christ, from the power of darkness and translated into the kingdom of God's dear Son (Colossians 1:13), I now render null and void all demonic working or effect that has been passed on to me from my ancestors. I cancel every spell or curse that may have been placed upon me without my knowledge since the Lord Jesus Christ, by hanging upon the tree (Galatians 3:13), has become a curse for me. As a child of God covered by and utterly trusting in the atoning power of the blood of the Savior Jesus Christ (Ephesians 1:7), I cancel, renounce, and nullify every pact or agreement I have made with Satan including blood pacts. I renounce any and every way that the devil has gotten hold of me and nullify any gifts, powers, favor, or workings in me which are not of Almighty God, or pleasing to Him.

I belong entirely and solely (spirit, body and soul) to the Lord Jesus Christ. I have been crucified (Galatians 2:20) and raised with Christ and am now sitting with Him   in heavenly places (Ephesians 2:5-6). Given that privilege I eternally and completely sign myself over to the Lord Jesus Christ. It is my intention that our Lord Jesus Christ will have full control of my entire life and to that end I will pray daily. I do all of this in the name Lord Jesus Christ and by His absolute authority over all things, rulers, authorities, and powers (Ephesians 1:18-23). Amen.

I confess Jesus Christ as Savior and Lord of my life. This is the same Jesus Christ of Nazareth, who was born of a Virgin, walked the earth in the flesh for 33 years and died on the Cross for my sins. He is the Son of God and was both God and Man while He was on this earth. He died on the Cross for my sins and He now sits on High at the right hand of the Father and is my Master. I am a servant of the God of Abraham, Isaac and Jacob. I kneel in total submission to Him.

Chapter Five

How To Prepare Yourself

If there is one thing that you need to understand about preparing to go to a tarry service, it's this. YOUR MIND IS THE BATTLE FIELD! Your preparation for the tarrying service is the preparation of your mind. For as you tarry the enemy (Satan & his demons) is in a constant fight to keep your mind occupied on anything but receiving the Holy Spirit. He'll make your nose itch, back hurt, you think of things like a snack waiting on you at home, the fun you had earlier that day, things you forgot to do or whatever it takes to distract you. This is why preparation is so important. Don't wait until the last minute when you only have time to get dressed and rush out. Get dressed and physically ready for service early. Now that you're physically ready, use no less than fifteen to twenty minutes prior to the service to prepare your mind. Take out special time to wind down. Be careful not to eat a large meal that night. Slow things down. Refrain from playing around and joking for a while. Turn off the television. The idea is to focus on receiving the Holy Ghost. Get alone if you have to. Start off with singing worship songs. Begin to feed your mind with scriptures that promise you the Holy Spirit. Here are some sample scriptures to focus on:

Matthew 5:6: Blessed are they which do hunger and thirst after righteousness: for they shall be filled.

John 7:38: He that believeth on me, as the scripture hath said, out of his belly shall flow rivers of living water.

Luke 11:13: If ye then, being evil, know how to give good gifts unto your children: how much more shall your heavenly father give the Holy Spirit to them that ask him?

Acts 2:38: Then Peter said unto them, Repent, and be baptized every one of you in the name of Jesus Christ for the remission of sins, and ye shall receive the gift of the Holy Ghost.

There are many other scriptures that will be helpful to you. Speak to an altar worker, minister or saint that may be available to you. If you like you could even fast the entire day prior to the service being careful of your behavior and the things, you allow yourself to be involved in. While on your way to church sing worship songs in your heart, meditate on the Lord and how He's going to fill you with the Holy Ghost. By following these simple things, you will be ready to receive the Holy Ghost when you arrive at the church.

Part Two

Altar Work

Altar Work?

This section deals with the subject of "Altar Work" only as it relates to the seeker. I could not write on the subject of "Receiving The Holy Spirit" without dealing with this aspect of "Altar Work" since they are so connected. Like the previous section these chapters are designed as lessons that can and should be used within a class setting on this subject.

Chapter Six

The Altar

What's An Altar?

Altars are raised structures that have been set apart for the purpose of approaching God in worship by burnt blood sacrifices.

Note: For the purpose of this book we will only deal with the altars sanctioned by God and used by Israelites.

History of Altars

Altars were brought into existence after the fall of man in the Garden of Eden. It is said by some that God killed the first lamb sacrifice to cover man's nakedness which was made apparent after his sin. Due to the sinful state of man it was now necessary for him to bring an offering of blood before God to cover his sinfulness. We see this in the continuance of offering blood sacrifices to God in Adam's children. For in the story of Cain and Abel we see people offering sacrifices. We also see that there is an indication that they were taught that God required blood sacrifices (Genesis 4:1-7). Why blood? It is because the blood is the life (Genesis 9:4) of the animal and the sacrifice represents our lives as well as the sins that we've committed (Leviticus 1:4). In other words, since the fellowship with God was broken by our father Adam, it was now necessary to reconcile the relationship through the offering of a blood sacrifice so that we could be forgiven and brought back into communion with God. Later we see in the story of Noah the first picture of what the sacrifices were placed on. It seems that they were not placed on the ground, but placed on a structure that was built by him (Genesis 8:20). Later Abram built altars in the places that he dwelt (Genesis 12:7, 13:18), Isaac built altars (Genesis 26:24, 25) and even our father Jacob built altars (Genesis 33:20, 35:7). Altars were made of different materials. Some of stones others were of earth and finally wood covered with brass or gold. There were stationary altars and those that were not stationary.

Stationary Earthen Altars

The first altars ever built by our early fathers Noah, Abraham, Isaac and Jacob were stationary altars. Whenever they moved to a new location they had to build a new altar. We believe that these altars were made of stone. The scriptures later teach us that these altars were to be built out of whole stones that were not carved upon or cut (Deuteronomy 27:4 -8). Whenever, there was a covenant or the desire for God to be close to them, to give His favor and blessings, you see them using the altar to facilitate this blessing.

Wooden Altars Over Layered

After the children of Israel left Egypt, the Lord commanded Moses to build the tabernacle, which was the method God chose for worship and approaching Him. The first thing you would see when you entered the gates of the tabernacle was the Brazen Altar. It was a huge altar made of wood that was over layered with brass. This altar was the portable version of the earthen altars earlier built. This was where all sacrifices were brought by the priest and burnt for the sins of the people. It not only symbolized Christ dying for our sins, but also the first work of salvation, which is repentance. For you could only come to the entering of the gate and surrender your offering over to the priest. At that point it is completely out of your hands and into the hands of the Lord. Following this is the Brazen Lava. This is not an altar, but it is nonetheless significant. It is there that the priest climbs in and washes himself as he sees himself in the mirrors of the lava. This symbolizes water baptism in Jesus' name. After they have washed and changed their clothes they enter the Holy Place (first half of the building) where they come in direct contact with the next altar, the Altar of Incense. It is made of wood covered in gold. Fragrant incense was created specifically for the purpose of burning as a sacrifice before God daily. These fragrances relate to the prayers of the saints (Revelation 8:3-5).

Where Are The Altars Now?

The book of Hebrews, chapter 10:1-10, shows us that, since Jesus shed his blood, there is no longer a need for the blood sacrifices of old and therefore no longer a need for the type of altars that were once used. However, the need for man to approach God has not changed. We yet need to repent of our sins, talk to God in prayer and also bring God offerings. Since that is the case we need to identify where the altars of today exist. In order to do this, we need to understand what sacrifices are still in existence. Psalms 51:17 tells us that "the sacrifices of God are a broken spirit: a broken and a contrite heart…." Given this understanding we can see that the altar of today exists in your heart. Therefore, regardless of where you are we have an altar. However, we also need a place to stand before God as we make our vows (marriage), ordain and commission workers for Christ, minister to the needs of the congregation in an orderly fashion and birth new souls into the Kingdom of God. For this purpose, we have designated areas in our sanctuaries as altars. One of these areas is the space in front of the front row pew and encompasses the entire pulpit area. The other specific area is the prayer room. So today the altar exists on the table of your heart and is also designated in specific areas within our sanctuaries.

Chapter Seven

The Altar Worker

Who Is An Altar Worker?

An altar worker is a born again believer who: a) works with the minister in the Prayer Line (the altar call), b) works with souls who seek to be filled with the Holy Ghost (seekers)

Note: An altar worker can be male, female, layman or minister. In fact, it doesn't matter what other office you may hold in the congregation, you can also be an altar worker. Unfortunately, not enough men step up and are not encouraged to do this great work. This is quite unfortunate because male altar workers are a vital part of this ministry. Not just for their strength to pick up people that have fallen, but to also to do the work as the lead altar worker. There are times when a candidate/seeker may have an issue (sexual, emotional etc.) where a female altar worker by virtue of being female is a hindrance to the individual. The exact opposite can happen also. Therefore, it is necessary to have both. Let us encourage our men, not just ministers, but other brothers to aspire to honor God in this way.

What Is the Purpose Of Altar Workers?

The purpose of Altar Workers is a) to assist the minister as he works with souls in the Prayer Line, b) be an encourager in the Prayer Room and c) do the work of a Midwife or Physician by aiding the seeker through the process of being born of the Spirit (receiving the Holy Ghost)

Qualifications Of An Altar Worker

It must be stated clearly that altar work, in spite of the great need for workers, is not for everyone. To be an altar worker involves much more than merely being born again. It is a specialized work, with its own set of requirements for those who have the right temperament and desire to meet them. An altar worker must a) be baptized in Jesus' name, b) be filled with the Holy Ghost, c) have a committed prayer life and be especially given to intercessory prayer, d) have a burden for souls, e) have the gift of discernment of spirits, f) be someone who loves worship and praise, g) be knowledgeable of the Word of God and h) have knowledge (training) of how to work at the altar and deal with demonic forces.

Appearance And Hygiene Of Altar Workers

Dress:
To allow the focus to be directed towards God, it is important that the altar worker be inconspicuous or modest in their dress. Remember we are dealing with mostly unsaved people in a very intimate situation and do not want to hinder or distract them with an unholy appearance.

Hygiene:
In keeping with the idea of not hindering or offending the seekers we find it quite essential to give special attention to our personal hygiene. The following are a few tips that are very helpful in avoiding embarrassing situations:

Body Odor:
Prior to working in the prayer room prepare yourself by bathing, using deodorant, powder and fresh clothing. Also maintain a supply of the proper items for freshening up for times when it is not convenient to go home.

Breath:
Odor: Be sure to brush your teeth and tongue regularly. Carry breath fresheners with you so they will be available for you prior to approaching the altar or prayer room.

Overbearing:
Fragrances: Sometimes a cologne or perfume with a strong fragrance can be just as distracting as someone's body odor. For this reason it is advisable to wear only the fragrances that are not quite as overbearing.

Chapter Eight

Responsibilities Of The Altar Worker

Usually when we think of altar workers we envision them in the prayer room laboring with souls. However, the actual occupation of the altar worker is much broader than that. They could be doing anything from praying and laying on hands at the altar call, teaching seekers how to prepare themselves to receive the Holy Ghost, to casting out demons in a prayer service. They are also prayerful as the worship service progresses. They pray for the preacher while he's preaching and the unsaved that they would receive and respond to the Word. In their basic responsibilities of "Teaching Seekers", "Assisting in the Altar Call" and "Laboring In The Prayer Room" they are a vital part of the church and a blessing to the pastor's ministry.

Teaching Seekers

There are a number of subjects that an altar worker can and should teach those who desire to be filled with the Holy Ghost. Some of these are "You receive the Holy Ghost by Faith", "The methods and process of receiving the Holy Ghost" (which includes Tarrying, Laying on Hands and the Holy Ghost falling upon you), "How to prepare yourself prior to the tarry service" and "Hindrances to receiving the Holy Ghost"

Note: See section on, "Seekers", for the particulars on these lessons

Assisting in the Altar Call (Prayer Line)

An altar worker must be watchful and mindful of the minister as he makes the altar call. He/she must also be prepared to go up and stand with him as he begins to minister to those that come to the altar, be prayerful and ready to assist in any number of situations that may arise. Sometimes he may need for you, if there is a woman candidate there, to lay hands on her (if you are a woman). Other times there may be those that are overwhelmed by the power of God and necessitating your aid in bring them back to their feet or standing behind them to catch them as they fall or assist when someone simply starts tarrying right there on the spot. There are also occasions when evil spirits are present and need to be discerned. As you can see there are many circumstances that may arise. Understand, however, that you are there to assist and not to take over. Unless otherwise requested always allow the minister to lead in the ministering at the altar.

The Prayer Room

Believers often long for a place of prayer where they can pour out their hearts before God and a place where many souls can be birthed into the Kingdom of God. When Christ instructed His disciples to "…tarry in the city of Jerusalem until ye be endued with power from on high" (Luke 24:49), they went to the upper room, a place where they could spend time waiting on God. Such a place is the prayer room. The fact is the local church is greatly benefited by having a special place set apart for Prayer and Tarry services. This room and its services are the life's blood of the church. For whenever you find a church with an inactive prayer room, you will also find that there are no babes being born of the Spirit and quite often no Spirit of God moving in most of the other services. If space does not permit a dedicated prayer room, the altar in the main sanctuary will serve the purpose. Time that is suitable for Prayer/Tarrying services must be agreed upon by the pastor and congregation. These times should be convenient for those who work as well as for the ones that are tarrying. A time should be selected that would not cause those praying or the workers to feel hurried. Once the schedules have been made, then they must be strictly adhered to.

Atmosphere/Preparation Of The Prayer Room

When you understand the importance of the prayer room and its necessity, you will then realize that this room/area is not just a special place, but also a holy place. For this reason, if a church is so blessed to have such a room, it needs to be sanctified (set apart). It also needs to be viewed as a birthing room within a hospital. These rooms are specially prepared for the process of giving birth. Therefore the prayer room should have a) a comfortable temperature, b) pillows for kneeling, c) enough space to accommodate the Saints comfortably, d) a supply of tissues, water and coverings (sheets and lap cloths), e) little or no through traffic, f) no on lookers or spectators, g) no arguments or non-essential conversations going on (loud or otherwise),

h) no telephones, i) attendants who will care for infants or small children preferably in another area or in the back of the prayer room and j) a thorough spiritual cleaning prior to the services.

Laboring In The Prayer Room

(Handling And Working With Seekers)

The greatest work done by an altar worker, whether at the Altar Call or in the Prayer room, is when they are helping someone through the process of receiving the Holy Ghost. Of all the ways a person may receive the Holy Ghost I have found that most have received through the method of Tarrying. Tarry means to wait with anticipation. When the disciples were Tarrying for the Holy Ghost we find that they "… all continued with one accord in prayer and supplication" (Acts 1:14) and "… were all with one accord in one place" (Acts 2:1). This insinuates that they were all doing something besides waiting. Furthermore, Peter states "… that whosoever shall call on the name of the Lord shall be saved" (Acts 2:21). It is from this that we have been inspired by our style of Tarrying for the Holy Ghost. For we teach those tarrying to either call on the name of Jesus or say hallelujah repeatedly while inwardly praising and worshiping Him in advance for filling them with the Holy Ghost. This not a chanting or emptying of your mind to get into some heightened state of awareness or frantic emotional state, but a simple worship that says thank you for your gift of love. During this process the seeker goes through stages and sometimes difficulties that you must be aware of and prepared for. There is "beginning the process", "conviction" (especially when it's their first few times Tarrying), "Demonic Oppression" (this doesn't always occur especially if properly prepared), "Force It" and the final stage of "Refreshing."

Note: It must be clearly understood that this is a birth process and that the time it takes for a baby to be born varies. Some births are quick and some take hours while others need days. Why do some come through faster than others? We do not and probably never will have all the answers, but here's what we do know: Some are simply ready, have no apprehensions whatsoever and have thoroughly repented. There are some people who have hindrances (see chapter on Seekers) due to events, traumas, or a variety of difficult experiences in their lives and yet others simply need time for their faith to get to the point where they can believe that this can happen for them. Many people are not in touch with or aware of their spiritual side and the Process of Tarrying helps them to get in tune with it. So don't be in too much of a hurry to get them through the birth canal. Remember the babies that normally have to be totally pulled out are those that are still born. So be patient and understanding because what we truly want are live births into the kingdom of God.

Beginning The Process:
Before starting the labor process the mid-wife/physician prepares themselves by scrubbing down and putting on special garments. So too does the Altar Worker prepare himself by putting on the garments of prayer, praise and also the Armor of God (Ephesians 6:11). We suggest that you spend at least ten to fifteen minutes praying and getting in tune with God. Why? It's because you are going to need His help. You need to have discernment and you need to be able to hear Him when He speaks to you. Now that you've prayed until you're in the presence of God (called praying through), gently approach the seeker encouraging them to begin calling on the name of Jesus. Remember all seekers have not the same personality. Some are contained and quiet, while others are outwardly more emotional. As they progress through the worship they will, through encouragement and their own determination and concentration on the Lord, begin to Tarry faster. Whenever this occurs and you notice that the Anointing is present, understand that the seeker is in the birth canal and are not as conscious of their surroundings. In other words, they are in tuned with God and Tarrying on their own. There is very little that you need to do except quietly wait and pray. Allow God to do His work. Normally someone who has tarried several times will move through the process this fast, but a beginner usually goes through the next stage prior to getting here.

Conviction:
During the process of receiving the Holy Ghost the seeker can experience what we call conviction. Where he/she may begin to cry and sometimes verbally express their sorrow for sins. Understand what's happening. They have come into the presence of God where they become aware of how holy He is and at the same time how unholy and unworthy they are. This is the same thing experienced by Isaiah (Isaiah 6:3-5). Many at this point get overwhelmed emotionally and stop Tarrying. Encourage them to continue calling on the Lord while inwardly thanking Him for His forgiveness and, in advance, filling them with the Holy Ghost. It's important to get them

through this stage because they will now enter the birth canal, the point where they will be Tarrying on their own.

Demonic Oppression:

Sometimes while laboring with a soul you will encounter demons. This is a normal occurrence when working with souls. Demons are very real and very dangerous! For this reason, we admonish that you do a thorough spiritual cleaning of the prayer room/area. We further encourage you to prepare the seeker by having them to repent and renounce everything that is not of God (see Chapter entitled "Hindrances To Receiving The Holy Spirit", "Renunciation and Affirmation"). Usually these precautions will prevent these manifestations. The only time this will not prevent this is when God wants to teach you something. Fortunately, the Lord does not do this often. Since we do not always have the convenience to take these precautions in every situation we give the following information:

Understand You Have Power Over Demons:

In spite of all the things you've heard that demons and the devil have done and the power they have you must understand that you have power over them and they cannot hurt you (Luke 10:19). They have no choice but to obey you when you command them in the name of Jesus (Luke 10:17) and it's a natural thing for a born again believer to cast them out (Mark 16:17). In fact, they even know your name and that you have the authority to cast them out (Acts 19:13-16). Remember Paul, the saint killer, cast out demons, Peter, who denied the Lord, cast out demons and even Judas cast out demons. In other words, you must understand beyond any shadow of doubt that, when you command a demon(s) using the name of Jesus, they have no choice but to obey you!

How To Recognize Demons:

There is a big difference in someone being under the influence of the Holy Ghost than when they're under the influence of demons. One of the main clues is the fact that a person under the influence of the Holy Ghost is very easy to handle. If they are dancing in the Spirit, praying and under the anointing or simply being filled with the Holy Ghost, they will give you no trouble at all. This is not the case with demons or someone simply faking it. When someone wants to appear spiritual by dancing in the spirit many times they start bucking or get angry if you touch them, but a Holy

Ghost influenced person is quite calm and easy going. Let's make this very clear. The Holy Ghost does not knock over benches or cause you to hurt yourself. Emotionalism and Demons do. When tarrying with souls, demons manifest in so many different ways that it would take an entire book to list them. However, we must understand that they always act in ways to hinder the individual from receiving the Holyghost. Here are a few signs that demons are present:

• bucking and kicking or acting wild
• refusal to call on the name of Jesus
• sudden changes in personality or mood (anger, fear, pain etc.)
• demons will not give praise to Jesus
• refusing to speak at all (dumb demon)
• strange voices (mean, nasty, baby/child voices etc)
• disfiguring of body or face (doesn't happen very often thank God)
• total refusal to cooperate (these are rebellious and stubborn demons)
• stiffening up of the body
• tightly clenching fists or hands in a claw position
• writhing or moving in a sexual manner

Where To & How To Cast Out Demons:
For a long time, there has been this fear of being possessed by a demon that is being cast out in a prayer service. The reality of this occurring is that demons cannot arbitrarily possess someone. They can attack you without your say, but they need your permission to possess you. That's why they attacked, not possess, the sons of Sceva when they were trying to cast them out "…by Jesus whom Paul preached (Acts 19:13-16). You have to open a door through sin for them to come into you. Otherwise they would have possessed the disciples when Jesus cast Legion out (Mark 5:1-12). It must be noted, however, that it is just as important where you cast demons to as it is that you cast them out at all. Therefore, we advise that you cast demons to the feet of Jesus for sentencing. Prior to casting them out it is essential that you first bind them (Matthew 12:29). Binding simply means that we restrain them for the purpose of rendering them incapable of performing whatever they intended. Putting it plainly, we do this so that they will not hurt the seeker. After binding them in the name of Jesus, command them (in the name of Jesus) to come out and go to the feet of Jesus. Please understand that, like Legion, there may be more than one

demon present. As they manifest themselves or are discerned, cast them out. Remember now, demons have no choice, but to obey you when you command them in the name of Jesus (Luke 10:17).

Force It:
Often we find seekers who have gotten to a point where they are tarrying on their own and the anointing is present, but they just can't seem get through. In spite of this they seem to be trying their hardest to receive the Holy Ghost. They appear to be forcing their way through. This is a very delicate situation and should be carefully approached. It can be caused by a number of hindrances. Sometimes it's unbelief, unforgiveness or even the idea that they need to pray harder or louder. In other words, work for it. Sometimes the right thing to do is to gently encourage the seeker while other times it's necessary to stop them and minister to them by explaining whatever is needed. You then encourage them (after you've resolved the problem that is) to continue tarrying. In many cases the seeker comes through a few minutes later. It is important, however, to know when to do this. This is why it is important to work with an experienced altar worker. For this knowledge comes by experience and experience alone. However, we must note that in any case, if a seeker has been on their knees for over an hour, we need to encourage him/her to sit up. Also note that singing worship songs helps the seeker after they've been tarrying that long.

Refreshing:
There comes a point at which the seeker is in the Spirit (birth canal) and you can see that they are not with us. They are caught up with God and totally immersed in the presence of God. There is no struggle at all and the Spirit is even moving over you. Do not. And I repeat. Do not touch them. Let them rejoice. Let them stammer. Allow God to take them into the Most Holy Place! They will begin to speak in tongues and the anointing will be present. Just sit back and enjoy the new baby. For they have just been born of the Spirit. Okay! They've just been filled with the Holy Ghost. After they have collected themselves you may ask them how they feel, but do not ask or tell them that they have received the Holy Ghost! Do not tell them they have received the Holy Ghost! Do not tell them they have received the Holy Ghost! Okay. You can ask what they think they need to do to receive the Holy Ghost after this experience. They will either acknowledge that they have Him or that they need to tarry again. You can

even ask them when they think they will receive the Holy Ghost. What do you do now? Rejoice! Shout! Get your praise on!

Helpful Rules For Working With Seekers:
• Be of one mind, belief and with one accord with whatever altar worker you are partnered with
• Stick with one seeker. Don't jump from one to the other
• Refrain from speaking in tongues while working with seekers (they tend to mimic you)
• Do not touch or rub a seeker unnecessarily (you will break their concentration)
• Maintain the right frame of mind (if you start drifting you could become a hindrance)
• When two altar workers are working with a soul, let only one quietly and gently encourage them (as not to confuse the seeker)
• Do not shout in the ear of the seeker
• All exhortations should be short and encouraging to the seeker
• Do not confuse the seeker
• Do not tell a seeker how to speak in tongues (allow God to give them the Holy Ghost)
• Do not tell them that they've received the Holy Ghost

Note: In regard to touching seekers I must add the following. There are those who are simply gifted in working with souls who constantly lay hands on seekers. These altar workers are very successful at helping seekers receive the Holy Ghost. I've seen them rock, rub, pat and hold the hands of seekers until they actually receive the gift of the Holy Ghost with the evidence of speaking in tongues. This is an exception to the rule of not touching seekers while they are tarrying for the Holy Ghost. However, I must reiterate that these are very gifted and experienced Altar Workers and not the norm.

About The Author

Bishop Steve B. Walters is a gifted preacher, author, teacher, advisor and businessman. He served on the Executive Board of the International Oil of Gladness Ministries (Atlanta, GA/Lima, Peru). A graduate from United Christian College (NYC) where he earned Bachelor Degrees in Theology and Religion and a Certificate for the Psychology of Counseling. As an evangelist he travels throughout the country ministering to both clergy and laity. He served as the acting assistant pastor under Apostle Lymus Johnson for the Greater Evangelistic Church of Christ in New York City. Bishop Walters is anointed to preach the Uncompromised Word of God. Especially in the area of salvation and in recent years has been directed by the Holy Spirit to write on this great subject. He communicates practical biblical principles in the simplest form so that every individual can be Spirit filled and experience the awesome power of God. As a Senior Programmer Analyst, Bishop has worked in a variety of industries including retail, banking, insurance, securities etc. In his position as a VP in the Independent Gospel Distribution Company IGARA (Independent Gospel Artist Radio Alliance), Bishop Walters has been active in various areas of the Gospel Music Industry ranging from radio, television, magazines, promotions, sales and internet. As an Actor/Model Bishop has been seen in television commercials, magazines, on billboards, websites and in internet ads. He takes great pride and has great pleasure in being the husband of one wife (Mother Sharon Victoria), father of three great children (Katrina, Steven and Jenise) and the grandfather of four wonderful grandchildren (Dorian, Malik, Tremendus and Peaches). He currently resides in East Elmhurst, NY.

For bookings, questions and comments about the book you may contact Bishop Steve B. Walters at: SteveBWalters@gmail.com

www.ingramcontent.com/pod-product-compliance
Lightning Source LLC
Chambersburg PA
CBHW070221180726
47999CB00016B/1146